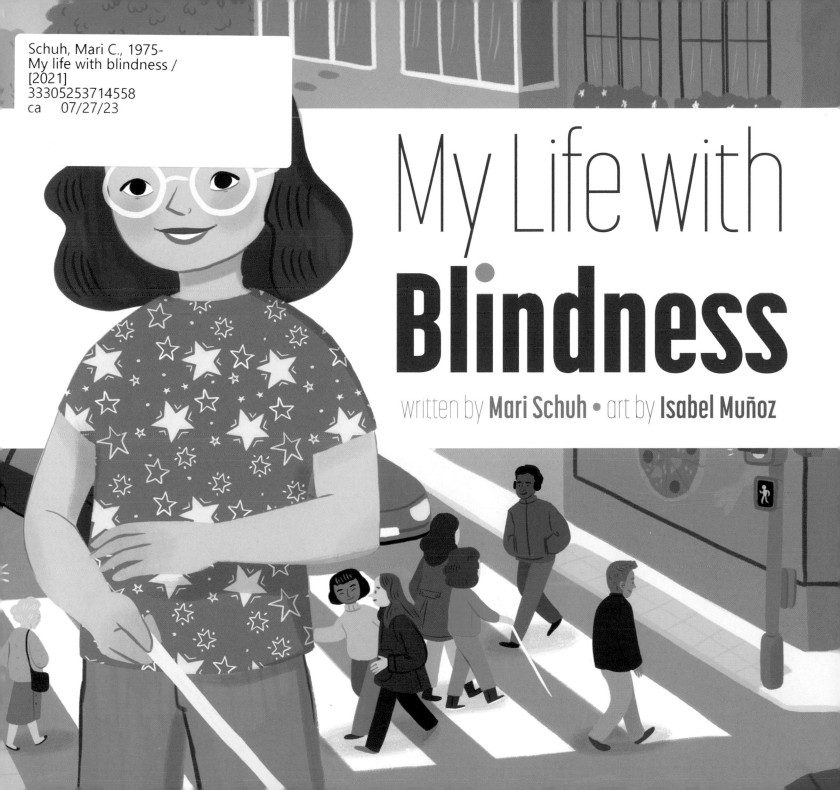

My Life with
Blindness

written by **Mari Schuh** • art by **Isabel Muñoz**

AMICUS ILLUSTRATED and AMICUS INK
are published by Amicus
P.O. Box 1329, Mankato, MN 56002
www.amicuspublishing.us

Editor: Gillia Olson
Designer: Kathleen Petelinsek

Library of Congress Cataloging-in-Publication Data
Names: Schuh, Mari C., 1975- author. | Muñoz, Isabel, illustrator.
Title: My life with blindness / Mari Schuh ; illustrated by Isabel Muñoz.
Description: Mankato, Minnesota : Amicus, [2021] | Series: My life with... | Includes bibliographical references. |
Audience: Ages 6-9 | Audience: Grades 2-3 | Summary: "Meet Kadence! She loves to bake cookies and hang
out with friends. She's also partly blind. Kadence is real and so are her experiences. Learn about her life in this
illustrated narrative nonfiction picture book for elementary students"— Provided by publisher.
Identifiers: LCCN 2019048127 (print) | LCCN 2019048128 (ebook) | ISBN 9781681519890
(library binding) | ISBN 9781681526362 (paperback) | ISBN 9781645490746 (pdf)
Subjects: LCSH: Blind children—United States—Biography—Juvenile literature. | Blindness
in children—Juvenile literature. | Vision disorders in children—Juvenile literature.
Classification: LCC HV1596.3 .S37 2021 (print) | LCC HV1596.3 (ebook) | DDC 362.4/1092 [B]—dc23
LC record available at https://lccn.loc.gov/2019048127
LC ebook record available at https://lccn.loc.gov/2019048128

For Kadence and her family—MS

Thank you to the staff at the Minnesota State Academy
for the Blind for their assistance with this book.

About the Author
Mari Schuh's love of reading began with cereal boxes at
the kitchen table. Today, she is the author of hundreds of
nonfiction books for beginning readers. With each book, Mari
hopes she's helping kids learn a little bit more about the world
around them. Find out more about her at marischuh.com.

About the Illustrator
To paint for a living was Isabel Muñoz' dream, and now she's
proud to be the illustrator of several children books. Isabel
works from a studio based in a tiny, cloudy, green and lovely
town in the north of Spain. You can follow her at isabelmg.com.

Hi! I'm Kadence. I'm a kid like you. I bet we're both different and alike. I have brown hair and I love to swim! I'm also partly blind. I'll tell you a little bit about my life.

I have a rare condition called retinitis pigmentosa.
It affects the back of my eyeballs. I see most things
in front of me. I can't see anything to my left or right.
When I'm older, I will lose more of my sight.

I love to bake. It's harder for someone who is blind to search for things. In my kitchen, all the ingredients are in their places. My family puts things back exactly where they belong. I can easily find what I need.

I read large print words because I can't see smaller words. Sometimes I listen to audiobooks. I also read braille. Braille letters and words are made of raised dots. I feel the dots with my fingertips.

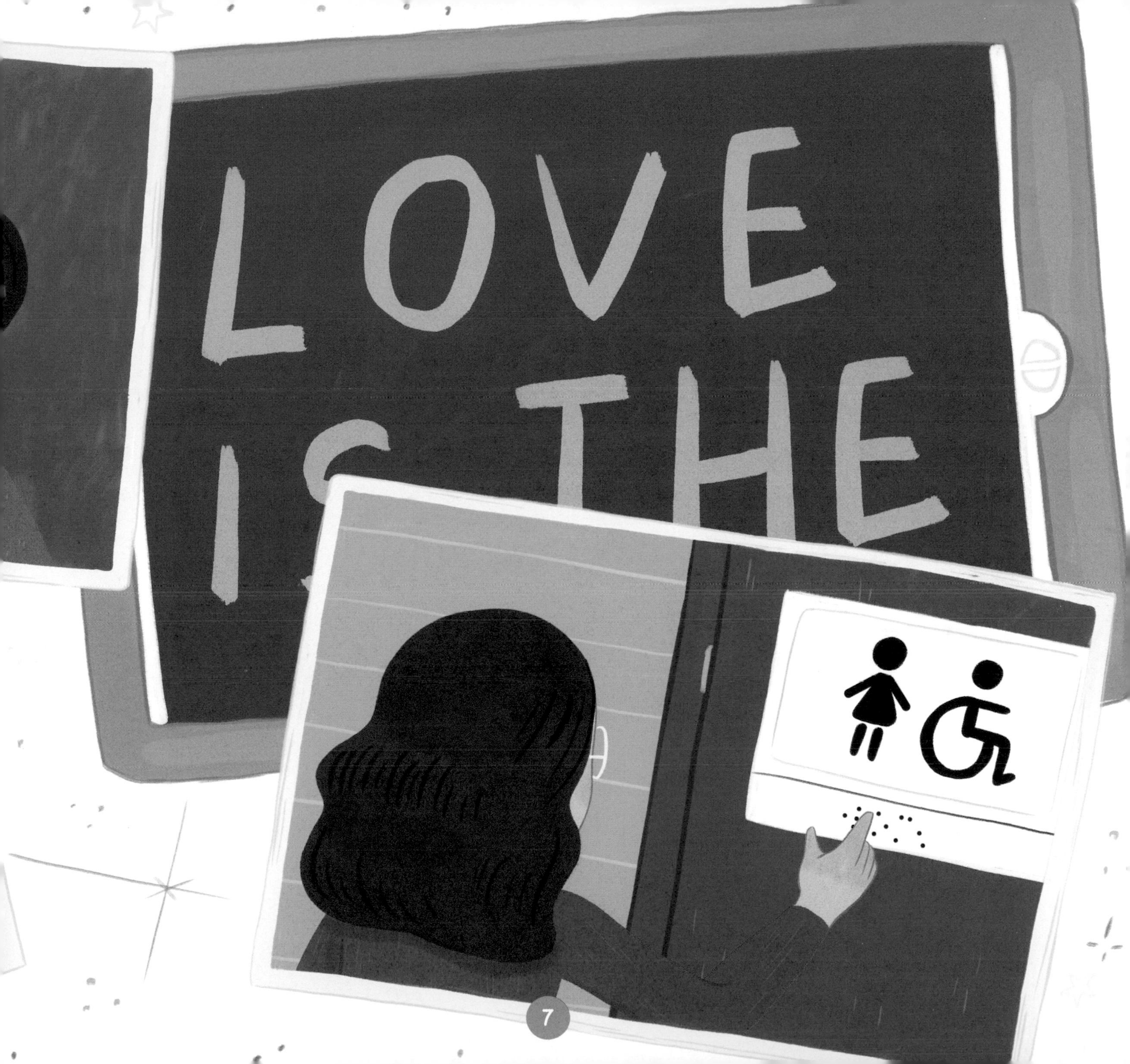
LOVE
IS THE

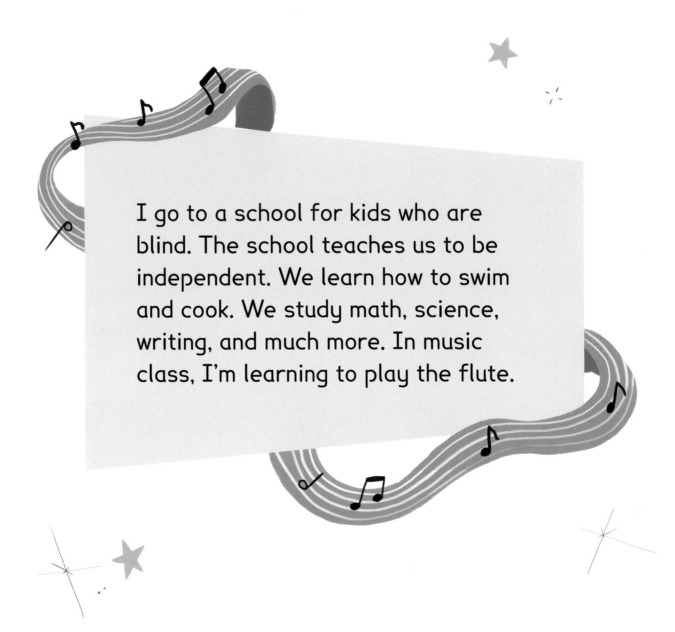

I go to a school for kids who are blind. The school teaches us to be independent. We learn how to swim and cook. We study math, science, writing, and much more. In music class, I'm learning to play the flute.

There are different kinds of blindness. Very few people who are blind see nothing at all. Liam goes to my school. He sees light. My friend Harper sees colors and shapes.

People can be born blind. Or they can become blind when they're older, like me.

What the world looks like for Liam

How Harper sees the world

Some days we play goalball in the gym. We all try to get a ball into a goal. We wear eyeshades so no one can see at all.

The ball has metal bells inside that jingle. You have to listen for where it is. It's lots of fun, but I get super sweaty!

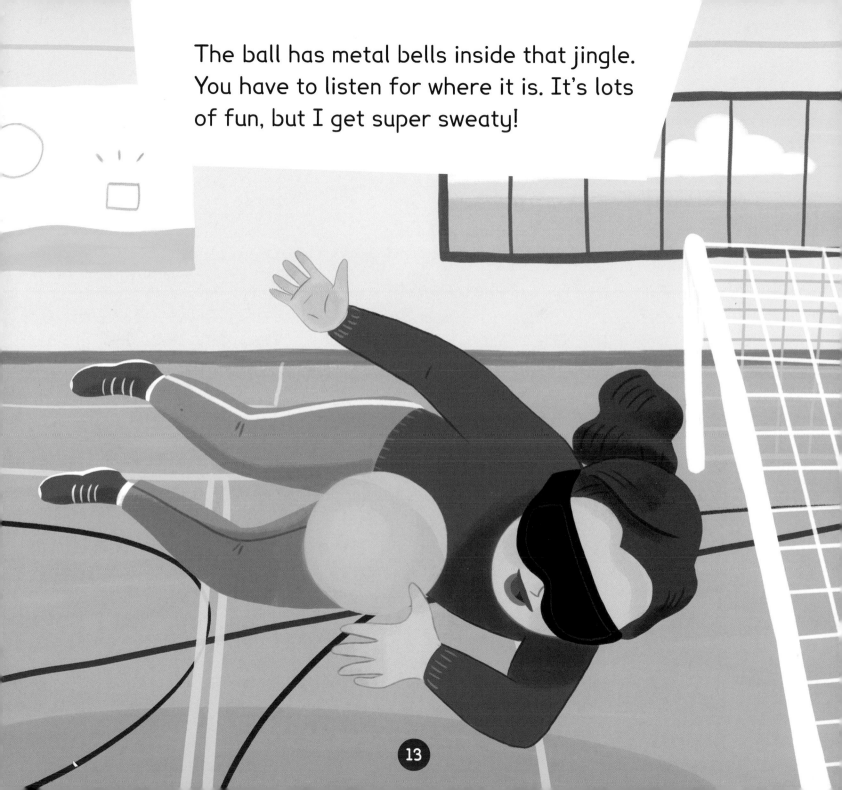

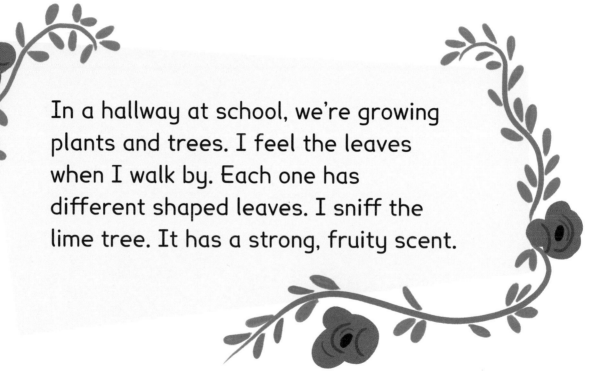

In a hallway at school, we're growing plants and trees. I feel the leaves when I walk by. Each one has different shaped leaves. I sniff the lime tree. It has a strong, fruity scent.

Yesterday, my class went on a field trip to get pizza. We used our canes to find our way and stay safe. We listened for cars. Bumps on the sidewalk let us know we're close to the street. Beeping traffic lights told us when it's safe to cross the street.

I use my cane only when I need it, like when I go to new places. Some of my friends use their canes at school. Others don't. I put a few key rings on my cane to show everyone that it's mine. My friend Lily's cane has fluffy pom-poms.

18

See that dog? He's not a pet. He's a guide dog. A few older students have them. Guide dogs help lead their owners safely while they walk.

Today, the weather is so nice! My friends and I went to the park. I'm wearing sunglasses because sunlight hurts my eyes. But it doesn't stop me from playing and having fun outside!

Meet Kadence

Hello! I'm Kadence. I go to school at the Minnesota State Academy for the Blind in Faribault. At school, I have fun studying. I also learn new things such as how to use my cane and how to read braille. When I'm not at school, I enjoy cooking, baking, and swimming. I also love to sew and draw. I like hanging out with my family, too. My family is big. I have eight siblings!

Respecting People Who Are Blind

Talk with a person who is blind with kindness and respect, just like you would any person. Look at the blind person when you're talking. Be a good listener.

Don't touch a person who is blind for no reason. Be respectful of them and their space.

If you need to get the attention of a person who is blind, gently tap them on their shoulder.

Don't touch or take the cane of a person who is blind. It belongs to them.

Ask before you touch a guide dog. Guide dogs are working dogs, not pets. They need to focus on their job.

Don't move around the things of a person who is blind. They already know where everything is.

Before helping a person who is blind, first ask them if they need help. People who are blind are independent. They can do most things themselves.

Helpful Terms

audiobook A recording of a person reading a book aloud.

braille A system of writing and printing that uses raised dots; many people who are blind read braille; they feel the raised dots with their fingertips.

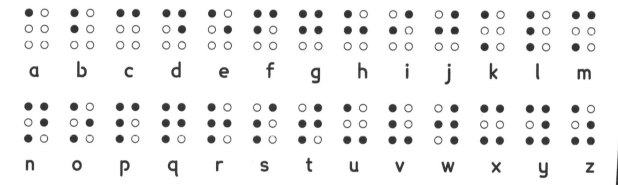

cane A pole that a person who is blind might use to check where they are walking.

guide dog A dog trained to lead and help someone who is blind.

large print Having letters that are bigger than usual and are easier to read for someone who has a hard time seeing.

retinitis pigmentosa A disorder where cells on the back of the eye break down; it causes a loss of sight around the edges of a person's vision and eventually blindness.

Read More

Chang, Kirsten. **My Friend is Blind**. All Kinds of Friends. Minneapolis: Bullfrog Books, 2020.

McDaniel, Melissa. **Guide Dogs**. Dog Heroes. New York: Bearport Publishing, 2019.

Schaefer, Lola M. **Some Kids Are Blind: A 4D Book**. Understanding Differences. North Mankato, Minn.: Capstone Press, 2018.

Websites

KIDS' QUEST: VISION IMPAIRMENT

https://www.cdc.gov/ncbddd/kids/vision.html

This website is full of helpful information about blindness.

MARINA'S GUIDE TO BRAILLE AND MORE

http://grownups.pbskids.org/arthur/print/braille/braille_guide.html

Learn more about people who are blind or have lost some of their sight.

THE NAME GAME: SEE YOUR NAME IN BRAILLE

http://braillebug.org/thenamegame.asp

Type your name into this website to see your name written in braille.